The Fourth River

JOAN I. SIEGEL

The Fourth River

Cover art by Jack Heller

ISBN: 978-0-9907958-2-7

Library of Congress Control Number: 2014950656

Published by Shabda Press
Pasadena, CA 91107
www.shabdapress.com

To My Family

Acknowledgements

Some poems listed below may appear with different titles and in altered form since publication.

Alaska Quarterly Review	"Archeology"
	"Blood"
The Bridge	"Autopsy"
	"Last Light"
Cimarron Review	"Black Cat"
Commonweal	"Arctic Tern"
Comstock Review	"Ancient Gesture"
Cumberland Poetry Review	"Spring Poem"
	"At Night"
Dogs Singing	"Dog"
	"The Dog Jack: Blind & Deaf"
Folio	"Getting Ready for Winter"
Free Lunch	"Afghanistan"
Hawaii Pacific Review	"Cat"
JAMA	"My Father Loses Himself"
Margie	"Writing the Poem"
The Mid-American Poetry Review	"Inheritance"
Natural Bridge	"After He Leaves"
	"Hands"
	"The Baghdad Zoo"
	"This Morning a Missile"
New Jewish Poetry	"My Dead Father"
Nightsun	"Scan"
Poet Lore	"After Divorcing"
Potomac Review	"The Fourth River"
	"War Photo"
Rhino	"My Mother's Piano"
San Jose Studies	"After the Funeral"
West Branch	"Our Father"
Zone 3	"The Last Quartets of Schubert"

The author is grateful to the editors of publications in which these poems first appeared as well as for the generous support of Joel, Emily, Susan and Jack Heller, William Trowbridge, Mary Makofske, Andrea Spofford, Diane Wakoski, Ronald Spatz as well as her editor, Teresa Mei Chuc.

Table of Contents

PART I

Ghazal: On Glass

We search for truth with a spyglass,
discover our names are made of glass.

In late autumn such light burns
as turns the world to stained glass.

If the hours take all, be careful
what you sift from the hourglass.

My daughter loves too much—
like Laura tending her sanctuary of glass.

All night the ice gods at their lathes
anneal the world, score it in glass.

At times I travel in the back seat alone
viewing my life through isinglass.

Birth Mother

I wonder what is you:

the gesture she makes with her left hand
as though a wild bird just landed
on her wrist

look in her eyes
as though she were rising
from a deep lake

how she laughs
when she jumps up
so sure sky will lift her away
earth welcome her back

Spring

Once more the world
pairs, pulls toward

the other like metal
filings to the magnet:

dances its wild dances
under the trees

breaches and arcs
through water

flashes its iridescence
into the night.

The air is thick
with animal music.

This Morning a Missile

His sister and brother.

Now he sits on the hospital floor. Waiting.
His mother, her face
turned his way on the gurney.

Long she'd told him
about the world's stillness, the river
murmuring through them all.

My Dead Father

puts his arm around my shoulder
and we talk to each other again:
we're walking down a street
it could be anywhere except
there's a lake in the sky where birds
swim past like schools of fish
at the crosswalk we wait for the light
to change then the sidewalk tilts
and we're running through the Promised Land
turn into an alleyway between
cement buildings where Hassidim
in red beards argue and my father
is a boy of five sitting on my shoulders
which the rabbis disapprove
as the sun turns green, falls
from the sky and rolls past my feet
but when I bend to catch it
it flowers into honeysuckle
my father is gone and all
I have in my hands:
honeysuckle honeysuckle

Sky Show at the Planetarium

Stars
shower us

we rise through Orion's nebula,
trail light years.

Galaxies spin off where earth clings
like milkweed in the black cold.

I rest my head
on my husband's shoulder. Reach

for our daughter's hand.
Our blood is thick

with stardust. Three of us whirring
under the dome of night.

Falling in Slow Motion Out of Love with Heathcliff

She was blonde
wistful beside him
in the grass.
He was wind-
tossed straight from the Haworth
moors, the gytrash still
in his eyes. That certain
recklessness. Distain.
She leaned
toward him like a willow
straw hair streaming
across his face.
Hopeless,
I watched from the dorm window
wanting only to be
his wild child   remembering
all the while how
the story ends.

Gilgamesh

Hilla
(March 2003)

The skies roared with thunder and the earth heaved,
Then came darkness and a stillness like death.

Along the scattered date palms
they come, black in their hijab
black as birds of prey, arms
outstretched like wings
descend on the coffin
with its treasure of bones
twelve years missing:
husband
father
son.
Their keening
shivers the dust.

Autopsy

What did they see
on the glass slide smeared with his memory?
A sentence?
His mother's maiden name?
A Percy Grainger tune
he played on the piano?
A birth?
His mother's face when she went crazy?
Private things whispered
or unspoken?
What he'd forgotten to say?
What he couldn't find words for all his life?

At Sunset

The sun split
wide open

spilling red juice
on the green corn

cattails   mullein
purple loosestrife

two blackbirds.

My Father Loses Himself

His keys
His words
His children.

When he finds them
they don't fit.

Where are my teeth?
Wrong words.

He searches
for clues walks backward
looking looking
for his mother.
       The boy he was:
hoists him on his shoulders,

jumps down runs
away.

Getting Ready for Winter

Sunlight like resin.
Our cat thickens his fur.

We pull sweaters from chests
stack firewood
seal cracks
on the north side of the house.

Fifty miles south
my mother alone in her room
shreds old letters birthday cards
receipts for what was paid in full.

Black Cat

The woods   grey as wolves.

      A great black cat   green eyes
      outside the window
      watching

On the stump of a beech tree
we cut down
because it leaned too close.

      All winter
      we burned logs
      in the wood stove.

Grey in his fur
makes him dusty.
He reminds me

of my father staring
through the grocer's window
hair disheveled   pants stained.

This April
air has ice
in it.

      We feed the cat but don't let him in.
      Dark memory:
      stays all night.

Archeology

Why assume that even if we are careful
not to break the years into dust, we will
break the silence of all she leaves
behind. Even as we breathe her smell
in woolen sweaters. Finger linen
handkerchiefs, strands of pearls. Hold
photographs to the lamplight, search
for family likeness in the shape
of a face. Piece scraps of letters pressed
like flowers between pages of books. Pry
words loose, turn them over for clues
as if we could actually find our way
back, know what it was really all about.

Our Father

"Our father is dead,"
says my sister

because she doesn't recognize
him anymore.

Barefoot in pajamas
one morning

he walks the streets
before we know he is gone.

"Going to Roanoke
to buy a pair of shoes."

He smiles where his teeth are not
and takes his fingers off.

"Let's go home,"
my sister tugs his hand.

"You look like my daughter,"
he says.

Hands

A girl of eight
like my daughter

the night before
music played in her head.

Wrap her body in
clean white cotton perfume

At sunset
hands stilled listen

to earth
to rain

Last Light

The violet beneath my mother's eyes
is the color of an iris that holds
onto that last band on the spectrum
before it is invisible as a membrane separating
one life from another
one hour from another
the distance between taking in the last breath
and holding onto it.

Entering

I push wide
the door opening
a dream   listen
for voices to guide
me toward middle
distance   freefalling
like Alice unafraid
willing to suspend
judgment of what

PART II

Doors

(for Marion Clarke)

"I don't like these houses
where you enter and exit the same door,"
says my Jamaican friend, cramped
in the August blight of a tenement
afternoon in Queens.

"In Kingston,
you enter through doors
thrown open like wide arms.

You move through spacious
rooms peopled with generations
of brown-legged children
and uncles at dominoes,
a grandmother stewing herbs to cure belly-ache,
a mother shaking out white linen,
a great aunt asleep on bright pillows
beside the window where
the hot breeze lifts the curtain edge
like a fan.

You move from room to room
slowly,   at ease
gathering the smells of mid-afternoon
and exit the back door,
step into the shade of frangipani,
the swell of hibiscus,
the sea carried lightly
on the air."

The Baghdad Zoo

*"Of the 650 animals in residence
before the war, only about 10 remain."*
—The New York Times

A lynx wandered Saddam City
outlaw.

Giraffe
in somebody's
Baghdad flat.

Four lions
went to Friday market
with Uday's horses

All
monkeys
ostriches
wild swans
slaughtered

All
Bengal tigers (2)
camels (2)
brown bears (2)
ponies, lions (3)
zebras, wild pigs (3)

saved

After Bin Laden

Bombs drop on his sleep. Both hands
fall off. Eyes go dark. Sister's
hair drapes poppies,
finery, a web.
Mother's arm sways on its broken
hinge. He feels his way over
steep outcroppings, bare toes reading
the ground like Braille.
Licorice root, coriander, saffron
on the right. Pomegranate, mulberries
to the left.

War Story: The Journey

An illumination grenade
opened in the boy's face
as he reached for brush
in the dry branches.

All night into morning, the father
walked from their village
to the hospital tent in Kandahar.
All morning the father leaned over

the unconscious boy, his face
a flame. The father nudged him
to waken as though he were asleep
on his mat at home, his chores undone.

The father leaned over the sleeping
boy and prayed to the God of Sons
to drain fire from his son's face.
He prayed to the God of Sons to heal

the flesh of his flesh. All day
into night, the father called upon
the God of Sons. Then he walked
into morning and followed it home.

Days closed, opened, closed.
The boy opened his eyes
and remembered sunlight
washing the windows of his house.

He saw an old man leaning
over another boy's bed. *Please*,
he said, *come talk to me
just like my father.*

Outside the Annex

"...the two of us looked
at the bare chestnut tree
glistening with dew..."

Bent over her diary, wrestling
a wayward heart turned
inside out like a sweater--ragged
seams showing, good side facing
in...holding steady to notions
of goodness.
                    He kissed her.
Their faces pressed
against the sooty glass   glimpsing
their future through the chestnut's
bounty of flowers--blue sky,
seagulls flashing
like a miracle.

The Diary

In the photo she looked
like my sister's best friend.
I was in second grade. 1953.

At recess the girls played jump rope.
The boys goose-stepped to "Heil Hitler!"
their fingers made a mustache above the lip.

A German girl in class
invited me to her house after school.
When we got there, I ran all the way home.

I'd heard my parents say Germans
make lampshades and soap
of Jewish skin. My father talked

about cattle cars, concentration
camps. I didn't understand. He said
the girl died. I cried all night.

Inheritance

She
never told
a joke

She
didn't
sing to us

She said
Don't laugh too much
for then you'll cry.

Daughter

You ran after me, calling
crying because I'd slammed
the back door, stormed
through woods as though I'd never
come back   your legs tangled
vines slipping over
dead timber
              caught up, you kissed
my knees to make whatever-it-was
all better as I lifted the full weight
of your two years into my arms
your baby kisses falling
all over my hands my hair
my tears   so many
kisses
to atone for.

Ghost Sister

The one we called from darkness
and named even before she lost
her way, clinging for weeks, blind
and doomed. Excised like spoiled fruit.

My flesh grieved. The wound
closed over like rind. Ten years
she climbed the swell of dreams
breathed against my face.

Ten years to the day
we found you, little sister.
She is not jealous. She watches
over your sleep. Keeps the gods at bay.

At the Railway Station in Yi Wu

I try to imagine the weather:
mid-October, still warm. Early
morning sky milky
as pearls. Air
thick with coal.

She holds you tight to the breast.
You watch sparrows circling
the station roof. You point, speak
in that voice only a mother
would understand.

No... not your mother
who is still asleep at home
her hand resting
over the warm place where
you were curled beside her.

Someone else... mother-in-law,
grandmother, mother's sister...tucks
a red card— red for good fortune
inside your jacket. It
says:
This baby girl
born year of Rooster

A cloud of sparrows alights
on the station roof as you tuck
your head in the shadow
beneath her chin. Sleep. Quickly
she stows you under a bench—

thieves away.

China Triptych

i.

Her body will remember
the girl growing itself
like a tadpole webbed hands
defining fingers   cartilage
growing into bone heart
building chambers thump-thumping
blood to brain lungs eyelids
opening closing in its amniotic
sea   body turning turning
to its mother's cries breaching
at last the narrows   flooding
mid-wife's hands with its new
self father's   mother-in-law's
disgust...*useless girl!* She begs
Don't throw her in the slops pail!
still white hot pain and pinch
of the cervix

ii.

A virgin she wants to feel
what her girlfriends know
a man's hands on her body fingers
exploring nape of the neck sliver
of collar bones   tongue tasting
ripe breasts curve of the belly
nest of curly hair above
the slit between her legs   she seduces
him   the professor who touches
her as she wants to be touched when
his wife is not home   he takes her

to bed once then twice and says
not to return or phone   she leaves
school   returns home to her parents'
shame and births it   hears its cry
holds it to her swollen breasts bundles
it in blankets kissing kissing kissing
baby girl's tiny mouth   'til grandmother thieves in
carries it off   leaves her to console
her swollen breasts.

      iii.
The mothers   you know them
by their restless eyes peering
sidelong at children in other women's
arms   you know them by their heavy gait
prowling alleyways   markets railways
how many footsteps   how many sleepless
days   weeks   months scouring
streets for the baby girl torn from their breast
baby girl with dimpled cheeks six fingers
a mark on her chin   eyes dark
dark as West Lake.

The Fourth River

Euphrates,
out of Eden
to water the garden.

The four year old wears a pink jacket
her mother's blood.

The marine's eyes, half-moons,
the darkness of a father.

Fantasia

The sky is pale as my mother's face, cold
as nuns singing matins in the chapel
by the river. Music slides down
her window like rain. It is not raining
but there is song and sunshine hangs
like blood oranges from branched
sycamore. It is winter but she thinks
of May. *Wayward feet will not outrun
the heart's weather,* she says. I offer
a cup of steaming tea. She only talks
to her umbrella hanging from the iron
coat rack: Next spring
rain falling.

What is This Stillness?

Daylight gone from his eyes.
Fingers stiff as candles.

In that other place,
jackals lay down with lambs.

It was always summer.

Here, dark weather storms in her chest.

This mother of sons
struck twice by flaming swords.

At the Window

My daughter looks like a red poppy
plucked from a field of poppies
sunny in the rain
the red hood of her jacket bobbing
as she runs to the car
turns
waves

The car pulls away
a thousand poppies in my red heart
where she was standing
where the rain falls.

Mother & Daughter

(for my sister)

Maybe it is not the words
you have waited all your life
for her to speak or
your own words knotted
under your tongue.

What matters after all
is comforting the body
bathing her
oiling the dried skin
anointing
face
arms and hands
scars on the belly
feet
an act of devotion
for both of you
which she may have forgotten already
which you will never forget:

how it was
after anger had burned itself out
and there was only
the wash cloth in your hand
warm water
the pale sick skeleton
of an old woman lying on the sheets.

Dog

Sleepless
that last night
obeying
the body's will
to unmake itself.

Feverish
she crept outside
to keep watch.

December moon.

Her belly bloated, pressing
into the snow. The body's waste,
freed.

Eyes begging,
look away.

After the Funeral

It rained later.
The rabbi said Kaddish
beneath the canopy.
We followed along
on our printed cards.
Flowers, a handful of dirt.

He told us not to look back.

At the house
we took off our shoes,
lit the candle.

A mother
two daughters
two husbands
two grandchildren.

We ate sandwiches,
waited for the doorbell to ring,
for someone---
a friend, a relative
to bring honeycake,
condolences

my father back
in from the rain.

Waking

Some mornings unfold
as a moth's wing drying
in the sun:

how the mind steps
from its chrysalis
speaking in tongues.

Ancient Gesture

When the official apologist offers
his country's official apology for
the errant missile that struck
this family's home, that flew

father and son out the window
like birds of paradise and the girl
smashed and splintered on her bed
while mother and mother-in-law danced

in the flames, he will say
an unfortunate accident, the price
we pay...dispatch a soldier to pour
dollars for blood spilled

into the hands of the women—
hands now raised in mourning,
palms upturned to heaven
as if collecting rain.

How the Spider Lures the Moth

to fold its wings
and follow tracks
sprayed gold and
sticky as pollen
along false petals
false stamen
false heart
false flower
painted ultra-violet
as the true sky

My Mother's Piano

At day's end
they lay it to rest
in my living room. I open
the copy of *Claire de Lune*
penciled in her hand, faint
markings.
               I hear the river
the light.

Echo's Lament

Now I am nothing, nothing but memory and voice:
voice recalling your last words spoken
last words spoken to a girl in a girl's body
body of grace in the leafy woods and streams.

My voice recalling your last words spoken,
woods and streams know I love you: I who am
body of grace in the leafy woods and streams.
Love, you don't know I almost died of love.

While woods and streams know I love you,
Love has fed on my flesh all this while,
Love. You don't know I almost died of love
while flesh-less I am become like you.

Love has fed on my flesh all this while
Love. You don't know I almost died of love
while flesh-less I am become like you
body of grace in the woods and streams.

Oh Love, you don't know I almost died of love
for last words spoken to a girl in a girl's body
body of grace in the woods and streams:
Now I am nothing, nothing but memory and voice.

After Divorcing

you want stillness
like a shawl

sound of milk filling the bowl

stillness
like a moth's sleep

a chamber

where you dissolve
grow wings.

What Can He Do?

who
floats up-
side
down
three days
three
nights
in the over-
turned hull
of his boat
some-
where
mid-
ocean
not expecting
miracles
breathing
what is left
letting go
of it
as he has
already let
go his
birth
boyhood
wife
hands?

In America, My Grandmother

At nine she leaves the Polish shtetl to live
with strangers in New York—Why alone?
So young? Maybe the sons already
delivered to the graveyard? I wonder
what keepsakes memory stows away
as the ship groans, tugging so far
from shore...how sunlight danced across
buttons on her mother's coat? Her kerchief
flapping? What dreams anneal her heart during
two-weeks' passage, jammed stranger to stranger
in steerage on the creaking Atlantic, chill
winds sluicing through wood? Loneliness,
vomit gripping the throat? But I know nothing
about the color of the sky when the ship
docks or who is waiting at "the kissing post"
to welcome her. Her mother's sister? A distant
cousin? What does she say? I need to imagine
a big-hearted woman with ample arms for hugging,
warm hands to hold a child's hands. But love is another
matter. Other children lay claim, she is just another
mouth to feed. In Brooklyn she gets jobs washing
floors in office buildings, tailoring men's suits, turning
collars. In time, she marries a tailor, gives birth
to my mother, 2 boys, 2 girls, one stillborn.
When the children are grown, she goes
to night school to learn English. Become
American.

Shifting

After he died of Spanish flu
my grandmother remarried
a widower who brought along
two boys, three girls to add
to her five in the Brooklyn
apartment where everyone
shifted to make room sharing
beds and one toilet and two
lamp lights to do homework
or mending. And I wonder, did
she tell them before hand
that the tailor named Jacob
was coming to live with them
because his wife had died
and he needed a mother
for his five children
and she needed a husband
to help support her five children
and it was a mitzvah that they found
each other and it wasn't a matter
of love but necessity and they should never
forget their own father but show respect
for the man and his children and maybe
love, a luxury, would follow
or maybe it wouldn't and so
one afternoon he climbed the six
flights to the apartment with his five
children and knocked on the door.

PART III

PART II

Black Bear

Suddenly, his black snout
among pale hydrangea.

I watch from the window, wishing
to cross over.

Cat

It's the wild in him
we want to touch:
ten million years
    opening
closing behind him
like valves of the heart
and the kill at the neck
is swift.

After He Leaves

she makes the bed
puts his socks
in the wash
slips from the house
to hide out in a motel room
TV plug pulled
so they won't find her
if they are looking
if they bring news of him.

Firstling

Suddenness
of blood pooling
on tarmac

legs folded
like ribs
of an umbrella

coal
of one eye
staring

white spots
camouflaged in dappled
light

branched
shadows

terrible
black frenzy

of flies

At Night

in bed
the lake restless under
its icy lid...we remember
warm water wild
frenzy of carp

Goldfinch

When you see it
on the ground, beak

cracked, wing raised
a torn sail, wind snapping

the feathers---you are afraid
it might still be alive.

Key West

It's summer
Duval Street
I'm walking
past the cafes
with my husband
of twenty years
all the girls
in their bright
tight bodies
short skirts
are blonde
twenty
years
younger
I wish
he'd slide
his hand
down
the long
curve
of my back
the way
he slides
his eyes
down
their
long
tanned
arms
hips
legs

Thirtieth Anniversary

        Then
you slept in a bed fifty
miles south, the monitor's
green light tracing
your heartbeats.

        Meanwhile
our house---a cave
of footsteps   twenty nights
without you

        Remembering
how our hands always
find each other in the dark.

Canada Geese

Touch
their wildness   sudden
uproar.

He knows they'll go
without him: high above

the schoolyard sunlight
flashing on white down.

He shouts *I hate birds!*
He hurls a stone.

Flails his arms: Icarus.

The Boy Remembers

She fought with my stepfather
and grabbed me
and my baby sister and brothers
and shoved us in the minivan screaming,
"If I'm going to die, you're going to die with me!"
and drove in the river and the river
flooded the van and she screamed,
"Oh my God I made a mistake!"
she tried to shift in reverse
I rolled down the window
I swam up.

My Mother's Hands

Soft as my daughter's hands
but colder
cold as the current
at the bottom of a river
wrinkled as the riverbed
but softened
by the river's washing
these first
hands that held me

Arctic Tern

He lifts
under the stars
tiny boat
the ocean
could break in two
day after night after day
halfway round
the earth
to a certain place
a certain hour of light

Dimensions

Afterward
The House broadens.
Walls push back.
Ceilings rise.
Your body hollows.
The bed widens.

The Dog Jack: Blind and Deaf

She reads wet leaves
for signs, dragging trails
fur snagged on blackberry vines.

All day rain,
the creek   spills,
washes
away tracks.

Night   coyotes howl
from the ridge   his body
electric   wired
scent
of the leash.

Scan

This morning was another place.
I woke to sunlight on the blinds.
My daughter's radio played reggae.
Our cat scraped at the screen door.

Now it is afternoon and stormy.
My raincoat hangs on a metal hook.
My feet are cold. The technician says,
Don't move. The engines start up,

drive me head first into the roar.
I leave behind my purse,
a sad mouth holding
my house keys, all my spare change.

Soundings

Roaming this lonely neighborhood,
we launch time capsules encrypted
with diagrams of man & woman
the map of our address
binomials
a recording of Louis Armstrong playing
"Melancholy Blues"—
our ear cupped to the farthest night, listening
for a reply
like that whale,
the only one of his kind,
twelve years cruising Pacific waters,
his tuba-pitched riff deepening
with age,
unanswered.

River Song

As the wild river singing its song of river
roots of trees follow their own nature
where the path to the mountain begins.
       While the canopy plays with shadow and light

roots of trees follow their own nature.
What was before you is then behind
while the canopy plays with shadow. And light
       tricks the eyes.

What was before you is then behind
and what you thought you knew
tricks the eyes.
       As darkness yields its own light

what you thought you knew
gives way like the wood spider's web plying the wind.
As darkness yields its own light:
       in light you will find your way.

Give way like the wood spider's web plying the wind
where the path to the mountain begins:
in light you will find your way
as the wild river singing its song of river.

Gayhead

Summer of the first moon landing
I went swimming in the chill
Atlantic off Martha's Vineyard just beneath
clay cliffs where long ago

native Wampanoag sent their children
to harvest clay among rampant
poison ivy so in time they'd grow
resistant to its poison.

I swam far out as fog wheeled over
waves shrouding me in opacity   purblind
I could not find my way   fighting
a riptide towing me farther   knowing

how twists of fate mark our time here
what if Apollo missed its rendezvous   Eagle
cut loose free-floating forever   no souls
of dead Wampanoag children to ferry us all home.

Two Mules

Grey as barn siding
they plod the dusty
tow path along a canal. Uphill
harness ropes strain, tug
snap between
raised shoulder blades,
slacken.

Thick muscles
unknot where maple grows
lush above murky water.
Between leather blinders, they look
straight into summer
chew
the day's sweetness.

And Again

The ease
of slipping a hand
into a hand
that made a good fit
the first time—
even the hand remembers
the voice speaking
in your sleep, eyes
looking
across a table
find what they
are looking for.

This Birthday

(for my sister)

You rooted first
then traveled alone
the treacherous journey,
making way for me later
as I put on your old shoes,
the tough leather softened
by wear. Now we watch ourselves
grow into looser skin, fragile bones
just after our mother has left hers
behind. All those years used up,
like the precious red lipstick we bought
with our own money and wore down
to a dried hard clump at the bottom
of its silver case.

Phone Call from My Mother

Her voice connects us
again. She forgets why
she called. Instead she tells

the terrible dream that swept us
into an angry sea. *You slipped
through my arms. You drowned.*

Here winter light unbends. Finches
splash in the oak tree. *It was just
a dream,* I say, pulling her in.

The telephone crackles. She is
too far and already
the lifeline slips.

Poem on My 50th Birthday

i.

Red chambered nautilus
my first room, dark
seabed beneath her heart

where I floated
in the salt tide lapping
my tongue before words.

ii.

Pain now dangles her from
an iron hook.

iii.

Soft as my daughter's skin
but wrinkled as a riverbed
cold as the river's passing—
these first hands
that held me.

Telling the Story

(for J.L.)

How she came home after work and noticed
the snow un-shoveled, the coffee pot
untouched, you on the bedroom floor bruised
and cold. How she rubbed your arms
insisting you *get up wake up stand up you are*
so cold and stiff how can this be? and stayed
alone with you to make sense of what
she was knowing before she called
the neighbors and later both daughters and
one daughter called the son who said
Is this a joke? and then *It cannot be*
and days later how that daughter wanted
to tell you about all the people
come by with baked breads and tins
of sweets and how they sat with somber faces
beside the wood stove rubbing their hands
because it was a raw, punishing January day
and the wind was whipping in the cemetery
where they had just left you
and the other daughter held her babies
close to her face and saw her own
childhood and wept for you who had said
my children are my pantheon and the grandchildren
did not understand why their mother
was weeping and why you weren't there
to ride them on your shoulders and how
it was the beginning of a remembering
they would always tell.

Songs For The First Born

(for Arwyn Rose)

i

You ride the last wave
of your mother's dark
sea,
drift toward us—

one of those puffy white
clouds bearing good weather.

ii

Your great-grandfather
would have danced you in his palm
through busy streets, humming
a Percy Grainger tune until the new moon
bounced from the clouds, rolled
alongside you.

iii

You will be
as the wild cherry
the caterpillar on its bark
the thrush on its branch
wind on its leaves
moonlight on its flowers
sap in its trunk
roots in dark soil
all bearing witness to itself.

iv

It is there in code already—
the outline of the story,

that you will
write in your own hand
color in your own colors
sing in your own songs
dance in your own dances
hold up to the light.

The story
of the river that flows
from mountain lake in the clouds
toward the open sea.

v

The world rests
in the palm of your grandfather's hand
the faint outline of veins
like earth's blue rivers
the geography of contours and ridges
just beneath the skin
your eyes reflecting the sky
at the blue gray hour
just before dawn:
the still point.

Savings

Against that time when my life
is an empty room,
drawn blinds and a night light—

I stuff my suitcase with this
Sunday morning when you are still
eleven years old in your red and black
penguin pajamas, reading a library book
and both of us and your favorite cat burrow
inside an old sleeping bag while busily
your father snores under the bed sheets and last
week's snow is thick in the woods where later
we'll snow shoe through fresh deer tracks in
a brush painting of black branches.

Already I have pocketed
your songs and laughter, pushed them deep
against the seams of my palm, the map
out of darkness.

Ghazal: On Sky

Gas lighters in dark streets of the sky—
these snow geese lantern the wintry sky.

What are stars but a silver service—
says Alice— *a tea tray in the sky.*

Fists of clouds choke the winter sunrise.
All day coarse salt rains from the sky.

What music was Van Gogh hearing
when he looked up at that starry sky?

Although the unblinking moon seems wiser,
I say, *the brain is wider than the sky.*

Warnings from Gaea

i.

There is no safety.
Flames lick the mountainsides.
Even the wind catches fire.
Ash rains like nuclear winter
on scorched bones.

ii.

Lakes shrivel
and shrink. Animals
lick parched riverbeds. Dried
tongues curl like wire.

iii.

There is no ground high enough.
Oceans and seas will rise
to meet you, fold you
into their angry swell.

In the Photograph

(for Susan and Jack)

These 49 years
One day to another

Each of you
In the other's keeping

On The Night Train to Marseilles

Through your reflection in the window
a woman embraces a man in the yellow light
of the station. You only glimpse their story
as the wheels push them into shadow.
You slide into night farther from home,
the past raveling along the track.

You shut your eyes to keep track
of half-forgotten things: the window
that opened to a pear tree at home,
how the room flooded with light
and high up on the walls a shadow
told its own story.

You don't remember the story.
Instead you look down the track
to the man and woman in shadow
who slipped past your window.
How you'd watched in the yellow light
separate, feeling sick for home.

But where is home?
You never will know their story
as you never discovered the source of light
or found a way to track
it from the pear tree near the window.
What was inside the shadow?

Between stations a man falls into the shadow.
They bring a coffin, carry him home.
You watch by the window.
He has a name, a favorite umbrella, a story.
He leaves a shoe beside the track
just when morning light

gives shape to memory. In the weak light
the dead man is shapeless. A shadow
on your memory that will track
you all the years you are home-
less. At the end of the last story
the pear tree taps at the window.

You stand at the dark window. Light
a candle. Your story is the shadow
following you home along the track.

Chopin Prelude in E-Minor

This page missing from the book of preludes
with their spiraling descents and
breaks of sudden weather
this quiet page missing ten years
folded in my father's hand
to take along on the journey
as if the dead really need what we give them
this music in a minor key
the mode of mourning
I know by heart
I feel it in my fingers
as I feel the sleeve of his gray sweater
what is part of me
his knees, his funny walk
the way his eyes look far away
I can summon it anytime at the piano
this meditation
my father listening in his armchair
there by the window

The Last Quartets of Schubert

In this wounded light
of late November
there is nothing left to be done.

My daughter asks
who will help her
when it comes my time.

Rooms emptied of furniture.
Floors swept.
Newspapers bundled.

How will she know
how to do this alone, how
to shut the door after

All the music's played.
All the words spoken.
All the window shades pulled.

Letter to My Mother

Early October trees already
tipped in gold. The sky worn more gray
than your old wool sweater.   Wind
at the back of my neck feels chill
as the string of pearls you left
on the dresser before you turned

your face away. Our lives have since turned
with the earth each hour and set already
with fourteen full moons and whatever is left
of this waning crescent. That August afternoon, gray
as rain, we shoveled earth's dust into the chill
bottom where you waited in that wind-

less place for the sky to close, wind
to worry our hair, rattle the branches as you turned
to life's other business of undoing. In the chill
darkness, light years of cells already
swim away to settle in the watery gray
silt where life begets life. What is left

of you intangible as music left
sounding in the flute, dissolved in the wind
and its ways. Intangible as the gray
shadow that sits in our matrix turned
inward, abiding, all ready
to unthread memory and bones. Render us chill

as your face when I bent to kiss you good-bye. So chill
I pulled my lips away, shuddered and left
you un-kissed who had become some other thing already—
one of the elements— Fire. Earth. Water. Wind.
My fingers combed through your hair so early turned
from black to palest gray.....gray

as that cloud floating across your eye, gray
as rain. My fingers hold that memory, my lips the chill
of winter waiting at the door. And when it has turned
its lathe of ice retooling trees and left
the nests of birds dangling in wind,
I will not worry you are cold. It is getting dark already.

My hair like yours, already early gray.
The wind toils inside my bones. Chills.
What's left of me will find you in the stream, returned.

Doppelganger

My father's eyes look back at me
in the rearview mirror
as the landscape recedes.

A reminiscence
tangible as the ghost image in a photograph
I never noticed before.

Maybe that is the way with the dead
who cannot stay where we left them last
and must come with us.

He wears my face like a mask
peering through two eyeholes
as the road curves from view.

I feel safety.
I could be travelling through the night
fifty years ago

curled up in the back seat
behind him
the motor humming in my sleep.

In Memoriam, William Trowbridge

(1941-2001)

Missouri Poet Laureate,
now that you are in
the other world having
left this one behind
after much deliberation
of the peculiarities of
our little time in the world
no doubt you are riding
your Triumph Sprint ST motorcycle
and tuning into those beloved
old Laurel and Hardy movies
while you dream up dark
comedies of life in suburbia.
Oh dear friend, you will be missed.

Time

Time ends in the gold
throat of the lily sipping
a last drought of sun.

www.ingramcontent.com/pod-product-compliance
Lightning Source LLC
LaVergne TN
LVHW041303080426
835510LV00009B/857